Contents

Introduction

Every person knows what it's like to grieve when a loved one dies. The pain of heartbreak knowing that someone you care about so deeply is gone from here on earth. You can no longer pick up the phone and hear their voice. You long to see them and feel them but you know you will have to wait until your day of entering heaven before you see their face again. Matthew 5:4(NLT)- God blesses those who mourn, for they will be comforted.

Did you ever think that you could grieve for a person that is still alive?

As an autism parent, I have grieved over my son more than I care to admit. I grieve for the things that he struggles to do, all the challenges, the tantrum behaviors, the isolation we have at times, and for what his and our future will be like. I grieve when he is in distress and he can't talk and tell me what is wrong. I grieve when he injures himself and I cannot console him or kiss his boo boo because he pushes me away. I long for that parent/child connection. I long for the world to understand the challenges and to have more acceptance of others who are different. As I think about all the challenges, the fact that every doctor or dentist appointment that we go to, I have to have my child restrained just for a basic wellness visit. Through occupational therapy we have gotten him to the point where at least I can give him a quick buzz haircut myself as the hair salon always caused panic, kicking, screaming, and having to be restrained.

 As I ponder about our challenges, I keep in mind our savior Jesus Christ who suffered the ultimate suffering and endured death on a cross in order that we can have a full life of freedom and forgiveness of our sins all because of his selfless act. What I am currently feeling or facing is only temporary and with the help of my savior I will get through all things. I can fix my eyes on the eternal instead of the temporary and hold onto his promise in Revelation 21:4(NLT)- He will wipe every tear from their eyes, and there will be no more death or sorrow or crying or pain. All these things are gone forever.

 Like other families, some days are better than others but on those days that are the hardest I need to remember who I can turn to when I feel in distress. Psalm 121:1-2(ESV)- I lift my eyes to the hills. From where does my help come? My help comes from the Lord, who made heaven and earth.

The Beginning and The Journey with Autism

September 12, 2014, I gave birth to a 9 lbs. and 21-inch baby boy. Let us just say he was definitely healthy. He looked like a 3-month old and did not fit into any newborn size clothes. After the normal couple days in the hospital we were sent home with our new addition Carter John. Being new parents, we were definitely cautious with him. I remember always choosing a sleeper with snaps or a zipper at first because I was afraid of hurting his head by pulling clothes over it, silly I know. We had big dreams for our boy. My husband Chris was hoping for him to be a football player and a military man. I, of course, was hoping for him to be into music as he had been on stage with me singing every weekend throughout my pregnancy, so even before he was born, he was introduced into music. I bonded with my little guy for my 6 weeks at home and then back to work I went at the preschool I worked at, along with Carter who I now had enrolled there. Watching him grow and change has been a neat experience. As he grew, I noticed some delays in his development, but I guess I didn't think much of it at first because he was just a baby, and this was all new to me. We did the normal routine as far as our wellness visits with the doctor and vaccinations, as well as a lot of sick visits for ear infections. My poor boy even had mono at one time, but the worst was when he had been bitten on his forehead by another child which resulted in him catching a herpes virus. After 3 doctor visits it was finally diagnosed and treated properly. I was so angry at that time. My baby now has this for life because of 1 incident.

My side of the family lives in Michigan, making it an 8-hour drive from Nashville. Carter's 1st Thanksgiving at 2 months old we were able to go home for the holiday and I am so glad we did because my oldest brother David got to meet his nephew. A few short months later my brother would pass away after battling illness for most of his adult life. We made the trip to Michigan for his funeral and Carter seemed to be that light to everyone during a sad dark time. After returning home to Nashville I started to notice some changes in Chris. The weekend after David's funeral I noticed Chris reading a small new testament Bible that a coworker had given him. Now if you knew my husband you would know that this was not like him at all. Me even mentioning church to him, I would get shut down right away. I am not 100% sure, but I feel like something happened through my brother's death and funeral that gave my husband that desire to have a relationship with God. My husband's coworker invited us to his church for Easter Sunday and I desired to go but I left it up to Chris and to my surprise, he wanted to go. We ended up attending this church after and at age 9 months, on Father's Day, we had Carter dedicated back to the Lord there.

Let us fast-forward to age 18 months. We arrived at the children's clinic for our 18-month checkup and I began to fill out the development of my child from which was a normal routine with each wellness visit. I had known for the past 8 months that there seemed to be some delays with Carter as he would never respond when his name was called. He had just started walking a month before our doctor visit and did not do the typical things babies do such as clapping and pointing at items he wanted. Although he attended the daycare I was working at, he always ventured off to play by himself and seemed to be in his own world and didn't seem to engage in group activities with his peers. He would only babble and didn't have any functional words. I remember the doctor coming in and reading over my form and asking me routine questions. Then the words that came out of her mouth hit me like a ton of bricks, "I can't diagnose him, but, based on these answers, he more than likely is autistic. I'll refer him to occupational therapy and to Vanderbilt for autism testing. " I got to the car and called Chris and then my mom to tell them what the doctor said. As I drove us home, I lost it, I cried my eyes out and felt like my entire world just ended. Our one and only beautiful son that God had blessed us with has a mental handicap, how can this be happening? He was born a healthy 9lb baby. How did this happen? Did I do something wrong during my pregnancy? Was it the vaccinations that some people blame it on? Then there was the fact that Carter had a ton of ear infections as a baby and had ear tubes so I wondered if he just couldn't hear well and that caused the delays, but when I'd recite a favorite book or do an Elmo voice he'd look at me and laugh so I knew he could hear. I soon started to research autism and my denial stage went away as I realized all the signs from hand flapping to tip toeing to avoiding eye contact, pretty much every item listed our son was doing.

 Chris had recently started a new job with a new health insurance. I didn't think anything of it as I took Carter into the occupational therapy center where he was referred. We checked in and had our therapy session. I gave the receptionist our new insurance card and it turned out we would have a very high deductible to meet that would have caused our first 4 sessions to be $200 apiece and the therapist was wanting to see him twice a week. I felt defeated once again as we could not afford that. Thankfully, the therapist decided to share some information with me. I had to call Tennessee early intervention services and put in a referral and she as well had to call in a referral to them, and if approved, he could possibly get some free therapy through them based on our income. After playing phone tag with this company for a while, we finally talked to someone and they set up an evaluation for him. It was a process, but he eventually started having developmental therapy for 1 hour a week. A few months passed and still no word about Vanderbilt and having the autism testing done so I reached out to find out why. Eventually the doctor's office called me back and there was a waiting list for 6 months-1 year before he'd be tested. You cannot tell me that my son is autistic and then tell me I have to wait for up to a full year to know for sure. Once again, I felt defeated and angry.

Fast-forward a few more months. At this point we had lost my husband's father unexpectedly to a heart attack. Getting that phone call around

2:00am, having to wake my husband up and deliver devastating news, and then walking with him into the trauma room to view his dad for the last time is a memory I wish could be erased. I was so worried my husband would lose his newfound Faith, but he didn't. After my father-in-law's passing, financial difficulty, and other life circumstances, as hard as it was, we would ultimately decide to sell the house that we loved and part ways with the state of Tennessee.

A New City, A New Normal

We arrived in Evansville, Indiana the end of August 2016 where we stayed with my mother-in-law for 2 weeks while waiting to move into our new house and search for jobs. While there, I decided to do some research on any companies that were similar to the free therapy services that Carter had received in Tennessee and I came across Indiana first steps and sent them an email right away. I knew the early intervention was key in helping my son.

The day after we got moved into our new house, 2 women from the company came and evaluated Carter and they determined that he needed all 3 therapies that they provided. Before October ended, we had an occupational therapist, speech therapist, and developmental therapist coming to our home 1 hour a week to work with him. Thankfully, I was able to be home with him and observe their therapy techniques and apply them myself the rest of the days they did not come. This was my first time being able to be a stay at home parent and financially it was rough, but it was a blessing as our son needed that one on one time to help him start to learn. We would sit at the table with simple flashcards, shapes, colors, alphabet letters and books, and would go to a park or the zoo quite often. About 4 months had passed since we moved here to Evansville and our turn for the autism testing that our new doctor had referred us to had finally come. We entered the psychologist office and went through the series of testing visits. Some of the toys she used caused some sensory meltdowns and based on his delays, it was determined that Carter did in fact have autism spectrum disorder (ASD). Now that we had his diagnosis, hopefully now we could get some help as our finances were a struggle as usual and we had these doctor bills that were growing. So, off to the social security office we went first. We were given the mound of paperwork to fill out and return. Eventually after turning in the paperwork I was called for a sit-down interview. I pushed Carter in there in his stroller where he sat watching Little Baby Bum videos on my phone while I answered a ton of questions. At this time, I had been donating plasma a couple nights a week to try and have a little money for odds and ends. I happened to mention that during the interview, and I was made to trace back donations so they could count that as income. Thankfully when I told them I stopped they took it off because it took away from Carter's amount. Before we had been approved, Carter was sent to the psychologist and speech therapist that social security had chosen, so he had to go through more testing which also confirmed that Carter is in fact disabled. Ok, now we have been approved for social security so he will automatically receive Medicaid. What a blessing, we are so thankful we are going to have the help we need.

2 Corinthians 9:8(NLT)- And God will generously provide all you need. Then you will always have everything you need, and plenty left over to share with others.

From Heartbreak to a New Friend

Going down the list of what things to do after your child is diagnosed with autism, I contact the bureau of developmental disabilities and get on the waiting list for the Medicaid waiver. Next, I contact Hopebridge ABA therapy center (who the psychologist recommended) and give them all the information they ask for and get on the waiting list. The waiting list sure seems to be a going theme.

At this time, Carter is around 2 and a half years old. We are rocking our therapy sessions at home with first steps, attending an amazing church where our son is able to go to a Sunday school class at, and on Monday mornings I take Carter to the library toddler story hour because I want so badly for him to have that interaction with other children. I know that the other mom's there can tell he's different. Their children sit nicely and participate in group activities while mine tries to take the librarian's book or spins in a circle and flaps his hands. I found out that the giant colorful parachute was a cause for meltdown, so on the days that was the group activity, I would simply wait outside the door with him until that part was over. I felt the other mom's stares to my core at times, and even though some Monday's I just didn't want to go because it was uncomfortable, I made myself take him anyway because I knew that was the best thing for him and I wanted him to be treated equally.

Carter's 3rd birthday came, and I wanted something that was fun for kids for him, so I rented a giant blow-up zoo, similar to a bounce house but opened at the top. I quickly discovered that this must have been a sensory no-no. Carter was terrified and wanted no part of that thing, lesson learned.

Now that Carter was 3 he had aged out of services with first steps and was transitioning into a developmental preschool for a couple hours twice a week and I was thrilled that I could go to the grocery store alone. I had forgotten what that was like. The next Monday came and we went to the library class again, but on this particular day, a lady came and sat next to me and was interested in knowing about my little C.C. (Carter). She was so nice, and we swapped phone numbers, found out we lived in the same area, and attended the same church. We quickly grew a friendship that has blossomed. This was exactly what I needed as over the past couple years I had become just a special needs mom and had lost a lot of my own personal identity. She had a little girl who was a year older than Carter and was also a stay at home parent to her 2 girls. Both of her daughters accepted my son like any other child, and he was included and it felt amazing!

Shortly after meeting my friend, I got the call from Hopebridge that Carter's turn on the list had come and he could start ABA therapy part-time, so we were on to a new adventure. He started his therapy from 8:30am until around noon, then I would pick him up and take him to his preschool twice a week from there. I learned right away that I couldn't use the school bus for preschool as that was a major cause for a meltdown, so I continued to drive him. We had our new routine down. During the hours that Carter was in therapy, I was able to spend quite a bit of quality time with my friend and I felt comfortable sharing my struggles with her. Proverbs 27:9(NLT)- The heartfelt counsel of a friend is as sweet as perfume and incense.

Adjusting Life for Our Son

 Chris used to always talk about one day he would like to move up into a supervisor position in maintenance. The time had come, and the service manager spot had opened up at his job. He was interviewed and given the position. Things looked like they were looking up as far as our finances. He was sent to New York for a week of training and given a $3.00 per hour raise. Soon I was turning in the pay stubs to social security at the beginning of the month as I have to do every month. The new gross pay was there which caused us to lose social security pay. After a couple months of losing Social Security benefits benefits, Medicaid was now not covering Carter as well because they go hand in hand with social security. Soon I received a bill in the mail for ABA therapy. 1 Month of part-time ABA after insurance was over $1,000. What typical family can afford that? Due to the loss of benefits as well as problems at work, my husband gave up his position and demoted himself back down to his original position. I, once again, turn in the pay stubs and we are able to regain Carter's benefits and I am able to make payments to Hopebridge. I continued to make payments with some of the social security pay but it was a stretch as that money also went to diapers and groceries. Finances have caused a lot of anxiety for me. At one time I almost passed out in the social security office while there to dispute a mistake on their part. Good thing I had Chris with me on that day.

 Soon I applied for one of the $500 vouchers that the nonprofit organization Autism Evansville gives a couple times a year. I shared Carter's story and sent off my entry. Soon after, I got a phone call, and we were chosen as a voucher winner. I was able to cover the rest of what I owed to Hopebridge. God is so good!

Philippians 4:9(ESV)- And my God will supply every need of yours according to his riches in glory in Christ Jesus.

 Our family has now been in Evansville for a couple years and we have had a lot of trials in our marriage. I had gotten to the point after bottling up hurt feelings for so long that I could not take it anymore and I started feeling resentment towards my husband. Thankfully, he agreed to go to a couple counseling sessions with our pastor with me. It was a process for me to forgive and let go of that resentment. While searching scripture for comfort for myself, instead I felt convicted when I read Matthew 6:14-15(ESV)- For if you forgive others their trespasses, your heavenly father will also forgive you, but if you do not forgive others their trespasses, neither will your father forgive your trespasses.

I definitely did not want God to not forgive my past sins as I remembered my party girl lifestyle from the past. That is a season I have no desire to revisit. It was a challenge but over time I was able to start forgiving and with that, the resentment started to fade. I am so grateful that things did get better. Parents of children with autism have a higher percentage rate of divorce and I did not want to add to that percentage. I want our son to have as stable of a family life as possible.

 I've had problems with back pain for a long time now and now that Carter was in therapy and we had health insurance, I decided I should start taking better care of myself as I had let myself go. Just standing in line at the grocery store would cause my back to spasm. I was referred from our family doctor to an orthopedic doctor who sent me to physical therapy and when that didn't work, he did spinal steroid injections. Well the injections did not take any pain away and these copays were killing our bank account. I was given the name of a chiropractor, so I went to see him. He diagnosed me as going into stage 2 of degenerative disc disease. When the price of the treatment plan was presented to me, I felt defeat. There was no way I could afford that, and I didn't have credit cards or good credit for that matter. I started trying to do some walking and was hoping a little exercise would "cure" me. I showed up for the next appointment that I was just paying visits individually for and before I went in, I decided I would have to just let go and let God and if I was meant to go to this chiropractor then it would work out somehow. Well to my surprise, this chiropractor happened to find it in his heart to give me care despite my inability to pay for the treatment plan. I got home that day and started praising God and I felt the Holy spirit strong and I started to sing random lyrics that popped into my head. After a couple weeks the lyrics were still in my memory and they became the chorus to a song I would soon write. I did everything that the chiropractor told me to do because how can I take care of my son if I'm physically struggling myself. I continued with treatment, started exercising on a regular basis, and tried not to overeat to often and with that I started to gain some health back, not only physically but mentally as well.

Jeremiah 30:17(NLT)- I will give you back your health and heal your wounds says the Lord.

Discovering my Identity Through Christ

Carter soon turns 4 and is now attending Hopebridge full-time hours from 9:00am until 4:30pm. At this point I am spending a lot more time in God's word and I have dusted off my guitar that I hadn't touched in a couple of years. Things at home could always be better, but in those moments where it seems to be such a heartbreaking struggle, I cling to the scriptures and read devotionals daily. Certain verses like Psalm 34:18(ESV)- The Lord is near to the brokenhearted and saves the crushed in spirit, seem to leap off the page at me and give me comfort in those moments. I start to fight my way back out from under the shell that seems to have become my life. I start to open up to the women in the small group bible study I have been attending and I share the struggles going on behind closed doors. It feels therapeutic to get things off of my chest.

Soon I start to practice guitar and start singing on a regular basis again. Sometimes I just make videos on social media and now, sometimes I play and sing to the dogs at the local rescue mission. I am slowly finding myself again. I do have an identity that is more than just a special needs mom.

The year is currently 2018 and the month of October is here. I soon learn that my husband's stepmother who I had grown to have a special bond with, has been placed on hospice after battling cancer for a few years. Within a few days she would pass. The trip to Tennessee for her memorial service was horribly devastating. Chris had surgery 2 days before and was unable to make the trip. The wonderful friend that had become a sister to me, made the trip with Carter and me. In the same day that I said my goodbyes, a close friendship with a woman in Nashville that was once like a sister to me, seemed to have dissolved. The desire to visit Nashville instantly disappeared. A few days later at my doctor's appointment I was placed on an anti-depressant. Thankfully, I was not on it for very long. I continued to reach out for prayer and support from my small group and continued reading God's word.

 For the past couple years, I had a desire that God had placed in me to sing on our worship team at church. After losing my Lou Lou to cancer and losing a friendship, I felt like a fire was lit inside me and I was no longer going to allow fear and uncertainty to control me. I was clinging to **2 Timothy** 1:7(NLT)- For God has not given us a spirit of fear and timidity, but of power, love, and self-discipline. I emailed the worship leader, met with her, and within a few months I was up there singing on the worship team. I will never forget the Holy spirit goosebumps that I felt the first time I sang in front of that congregation. I had sung a lot in the past as far as festivals, bars in Nashville, and had even made an album in my younger days, but none of that compared to what I felt singing for God. I felt like I was at home, where I should have been singing all along.

1 Peter 4:10(NLT)- God had given each of you a gift from his great variety of spiritual gifts. Use them well to serve one another.

Overcoming Life's Obstacles with Faith

The year is now 2019 and I am keeping busy with taking care of Carter, volunteering at my church, and studying God's word. I try to donate plasma as we battle financial struggles but most days my protein levels are too low despite the amount of protein I'm taking in, so I continue to be turned away from donating. Once again, I feel defeated for a moment but I keep on going. July is here and our family dog Maggie May takes a turn for the worse. Ultimately the decision is left up to me and I cannot bear to watch her suffer anymore. July 29, 2019, we take her into the vet for the very last time. I felt like I lost a part of my heart that day. Less than a week later I decided to try fostering a puppy. Let's just say a small puppy is not a good fit for our autism household. Suddenly there was this adorable but needy pup in the house that was chasing Carter and nipping at his toes. The intensity of his meltdowns grew, and he became destructive, tearing apart our shade, running through the house in hysterics.

 While the puppy was still with us, I became very ill and thought it was the flu. My temperature the first day was 104° so I went to the walk-in clinic. It was determined that I did not have the flu. I was given anti-nausea medication and sent home. The next morning, I awoke to the worst headache I had ever felt, chills, and this time there was blood in my stool. I checked my temperature and it read 106.9°. Wow! I didn't know your temp could get that high and I felt delusional. Chris called into work to take care of Carter and get him to therapy while my friend quickly drove me to the emergency room. After I.V. fluids, tests, and a cat scan of my abdomen, it was determined that I had an infection in my colon (colitis). Through I.V. fluids and Tylenol my temperature finally got to normal and I was able to go home with a bunch of meds. I got settled in at home and my friend brought the puppy back to the rescue for me. Taking time to heal with autism fits in the mix was certainly not an easy task but with diet changes and faith, after about a month I started to feel somewhat normal again. I soon got back into the gym I had joined a year prior and had gotten 20 lbs. lighter. After getting sick another 10 lbs. came off and I hit a 30 lb. weight loss. The routine of staying active with some weight loss helped some of that back pain. The scale is sometimes a struggle because like most people, I like tasty foods, but God has helped me to stay self-disciplined and given me the strength to persevere.

Lamentations 3:22-23(ESV)- The steadfast love of the Lord never ceases; his mercies never come to an end; they are new every morning; great is your faithfulness.

A Deeper Relationship

It is summer 2019 and our church starts offering a Wednesday morning women's bible study. It starts right after I drop Carter off, so the timing is perfect. I have never done this before, and I feel a little anxious going by myself, but I am determined to not backslide in my faith or how far I've come in getting out of my shell. I go in there with my brave face on and quickly recognize a couple people and I feel more at ease. I know that I want to learn more, so I keep myself self-disciplined and I do the daily homework assignment. The more of these studies I do, the more I am soul searching and really digging deep and the more I feel myself starting to grow in my relationship with Christ. I'm clinging to Philippians 4:13(ESV)- I can do ALL things through him who strengthens me. Soon I am chiming in and answering and sharing with the group. Where did this courage come from? I know in my own strength I could not do this. I feel so refreshed and just peaceful.

God soon starts to put things on my heart. After struggling financially for so long the idea of cleaning homes comes to mind. I do not submit to his calling right away because I am just a little unsure. I mention it to our small group leader and right away she tells me she's been wanting someone to clean for her once a month, so she becomes my first home. Inspired by the amazing woman she is and how deep of a relationship with Christ she has, I look up to her as an amazing mentor. I leave a bible scripture on her cleaning checklist for encouragement. A couple months pass and before I know it, I have more homes to clean. I submitted to God and he opened the door and blessed me with this, and I honor him by working as I am working for him (Colossians 3:23). Who would have thought that I'd ever be able to say that I'm "self-employed"? After working for several companies in the past, some of which caused severe stress and anxiety, I am finally in a pretty peaceful position all because of God's calling.

1 Chronicles 16:34(NLT)- Give thanks to the Lord, for he is good! His faithful love endures forever.

Making Allowance for Others

2019 is ending and it's been almost 3 years since we received Carter's autism diagnosis. I have gotten pretty used to him not always being treated equally by some people because he is not the "typical" child. At times when I talk about his behavior to a loved one, the subject is quickly changed, or I have heard things like "maybe he'll grow out of that one day." I guess sometimes denial is just easier. I used to always get angry, and don't get me wrong, it still hurts feeling left out, but with faith and a relationship with Christ, I've gotten better at letting go of a lot of that built up anger. I try to apply Colossians 3:13(NLT)- Make allowance for each other's faults and forgive anyone who offends you. Remember, the Lord forgave you, so you must forgive others.

At this point, we have been trying off and on to potty train for the last few years with not much success as potty training a fairly non-verbal child is definitely a challenge. One of the other parents at Hopebridge sees me carrying in a case of store bought pull-ups and brings it to my attention that with our Medicaid we can receive free medical diapers and she gives me the information I need. I am so thankful for this because not only are they expensive, but Carter is outgrowing the sizes in the store. Who would have thought free diapers could cause so much happiness. I felt like I won the lottery. Always count every blessing big and small. Ephesians 5:20(NLT)- And give thanks for everything to God the father in the name of our Lord Jesus Christ.

Having a child with special needs really brings awareness about the things most others take for granted. I would love to take my son out to an old-fashioned ice cream shop on a hot summer day but due to sensory issues, he does not like ice cream or popsicles. What kid doesn't like frozen treats? Most kids like french fries, chicken nuggets, and hamburgers. Mine will not eat any of those things. Even when traveling to Michigan to visit the family, I have to pack his normal lunch which consists of a peanut butter and jelly sandwich, chips, grapes, and an applesauce pouch. He will only eat applesauce in a pouch. If you put it in a bowl with a spoon, he will look disgusted and shove it away. Every night dinner is either pizza or mini pancakes and sometimes if he is in a bad behavior mood, he will refuse to eat that. Quite often I feel aggravated at the food difficulties. I pretty much have to buy Carter his own set of groceries. I've heard the phrase so many times "If he gets hungry enough, he'll eat." No, he will not! It does not matter how hungry he is, he will refuse to eat anything I cook unless it is pizza. I definitely don't want my son to end up malnourished, and as stubborn as he is, as a mom I don't want him to go to bed hungry so quite often I give in and offer a banana or chips because I know he'll eat that because they are favorites of his. But other than food, everything else also seems to be a challenge. At age 5 I am still applying the hand over hand method to wash hands and brush teeth for self-care. He cannot get dressed without assistance and cannot verbally tell me how he is feeling. I have not attempted to take him grocery shopping with me in a long time because he is too big for me to lift and put in the seat of the cart. He will not simply walk next to me but will run (ABA calls this eloping). When he runs, he does not pay attention to where he's running to. I don't think I'll ever be ready for him to wander off in public, so when we are somewhere public, I have a nice grip on his little hand or we still use a stroller because I know he can't get away from me. The stroller also has been handy because sometimes Carter will flop to the ground and refuse to walk. I sometimes worry about his future, as far as what will happen when Chris and I are passed on. Who will take care of him as he is an only child? Will he get to a point eventually where he can function on more of a normal level? Will he be in an assisted living home when he is an adult? I have even thought about how I will more than likely never be able to be a grandma one day and that breaks my heart. But I cannot live my life in fear of what the future may or may not bring.

Matthew 6:34(NLT)- So do not worry about tomorrow, for tomorrow will bring its own worries. Today's trouble is enough for today.

Peace and Manna

We are now entering the year 2020 and it was recently brought to my attention that a lot of Carter's newer defiant behaviors are showing signs of oppositional defiance disorder (ODD). After a meeting with his BCBA therapist at Hopebridge, I call around to the psychiatric clinics that she referred. I finally get an appointment scheduled at one and find out it will be $300 for the ODD testing as they do not accept his Medicaid. I plan the $300 out in our budget because we need answers and a plan as his aggression has gotten a little worse. We show up for our appointment the beginning of March and go through the normal paperwork routine and are brought into the psychiatrist's office and asked a series of questions. After describing to him Carter's behaviors, he decides that the behaviors still fall under the umbrella of autism and because Carter is young, he does not want to do the testing on him. I felt very discouraged leaving with no more answers than I had arrived with. We reached out to a professional for help and were unable to get that help. Why is it so hard to get a secondary diagnosis? I feel upset for the rest of the day but because of the amazing God that I serve, he supplied me with the peace that passes understanding (**Philippians** 4:7), and I was able to simply move on.

At this point we have a new family dog that we adopted in January. While singing to the rescue dogs I came across one in the back kennel that quickly caught my attention. As the other dogs were barking and carrying on, this particular one was laying on her cot quietly watching me sing to her. She never barked at me, just laid there timidly watching me. I was there with my friend who volunteers and we were getting ready to leave and I had this instant gut feeling that I had to do a meet and greet with this dog before we left, which I normally didn't do. Now it had been around 6 months since our Maggie had passed and we felt like we were ready for another dog once the right one came along. I took this as a sign from God and Chris and I went back the next day and brought her home to foster overnight and see how she would do in our autism home. She did great and Carter did not seem to mind her being there so the next day we went back and adopted her. Feeling like she was God sent, I wanted to honor that, so she was renamed Manna (from heaven). She is normally ready and willing to sit in my lap and give cuddles and affection which I can always use. I try and get those hugs and cuddles from Carter but quite often he pushes me away. Occasionally when he does hug back or I can get him to repeat "I love you", those moments fill my heart to overflowing. I am sure I probably get on his nerves at times with my affection, but I cannot accept not loving on him. I will never give up when it comes to showing him love.

Proverbs 22:6(ESV)- Train up a child in the way he should go; even when he is old, he will not depart from it.

From Pandemic to Quality Time

About a week after Carter's appointment with the psychiatrist, everything shut down due to the covid-19 pandemic, including Hopebridge. Knowing that Carter would be home full-time was a little concerning as we did not want him to backslide in the progress he had been making. While there was a lot of panic going on everywhere, I seemed to feel at peace despite the circumstances. It is amazing how God can put that peace in you. I soon was contacted by Carter's BCBA and the option of using zoom to facetime became available. This was new to us, as I am not the most tech savvy person, but we figured it out and soon we were having occupational and speech therapies through a facetime approach. I got Carter on a schedule here at home similar to his therapy center. We worked on asking for our food items, dressing,

tracing shapes, etc. and spent time dancing and
going for walks in the stroller or wagon. When
the weather allowed, we would play outside. It
is kind of brought me back to the younger
Carter, first steps therapy days. I think the break
was just what he needed at the time because his
fits were not too bad, and I enjoyed my time
with him. Soon the women's bible study was
also going through zoom, so I was able to
complete the current study we were in which
kept me busy and kept me in God's word.

It was now April and Easter Sunday were here.
Despite not being able to physically go to
church, we still wore our Sunday best and
watched church service online. I cooked a big
Easter dinner just for our little family, well for
Chris and me, as Carter, like most kids on the
spectrum will only eat a few items, so he had his
normal everyday lunch. After we ate, we did an
Easter egg hunt in the backyard. We have to
help him with this by guiding him to the eggs. I
have always done all the "traditional" things
with Carter because I feel that it is important for

him to get to experience those things just like other kids.

 The next day comes and I find out that Hopebridge will reopen on that Tuesday and slowly bring small groups of kids back in with all the necessary steps to be as safe as possible, so Carter is in the 1st group of patients to return. I am thankful that he can get back to a normal routine and I can have a much-needed break. Matthew 11:28(NLT)- Then Jesus said, "Come to me, all of you who are weary and carry heavy burdens, and I will give you rest."

Psalm 91

Our church is currently having a drive-in service in the parking lot and online services, so everything is still closed down at this point. I reach out for a little prayer on the Tuesday that Carter goes back to Hopebridge from my women's small group and I am sent Psalm 91. I did not sleep much the night before because deep down, I am a little concerned sending Carter back with the risk of this pandemic. I am so thankful for these ladies! Knowing that these God-fearing women are praying with me, it calms my anxiety. I sit on Carter's bed before waking him and read Psalm 91 out loud.

 I notice at this point, that our small group leader has not chimed in much lately and her health has taken a turn after battling cancer for so long. After a handful of days, I would get the call that she had passed. Plans for her memorial and funeral were made, but due to the pandemic, it was a closed funeral. We made bright colored signs to encourage her family and attended from the parking lot and were able to watch the service through social media. Knowing that she was gone here on earth was devastating but knowing that she was in heaven where we all long to be one day, brought comfort and peace. Although there were now changes and our group was missing our amazing leader, we continued on as a group bringing encouragement to each other and continuing to study God's word together. Despite the pandemic, our group was able to start meeting again in person, distancing the best we could. I am so thankful for our community group and what each person brings. I can feel the Holy spirit as we bow in prayer. He brings peace and a sense of comfort when we need it the most. Psalm 29:11(NLT)- The Lord gives his people strength. The Lord blesses them with peace.

New Behaviors

It is now summertime and we are spending a lot of time in Carter's shallow blow-up pool. Water seems to be his favorite as well as mine. I hope to one day get him some swimming lessons with someone who works with special needs, as at this point, Carter does not seem to have a sense of danger. He has only been in a big pool a handful of times with his puddle jumper life jacket securely in place.

At this point, our church is re-opened with restrictions. We decided to attend with Carter. The first few times he does great. He seems to enjoy the worship music as he flaps his hands and squeals. Once the sermon starts, he watches the color crew cartoon on my phone on silent to try and keep him calm. One Sunday while Chris is working, I decide to take him to church by myself. The first song starts, and he seems to be dancing and enjoying it. The second song starts, and he begins to drop to the floor and scream.

After a couple of tries, I scoop him up and exit quickly because I do not want to cause a scene in the middle of church. We get home and it is melt down city. At this point it seems like his behaviors are starting to get worse. Chris and I both notices how sometimes he will go from a fit of rage to smiling and happy like someone just flipped a switch. We both are wondering if he may have some bi-polar disorder as children with autism are at a higher risk for having other disorders. Even though he has not had an official diagnosis, we have also noticed some obsessive-compulsive disorder (OCD) tendencies as well.

 We are now awaiting an appointment with the psychologist who diagnosed his autism to see if we can get some answers and a treatment plan moving forward. Like most offices, there is a waitlist. I decided to call and reach out for an appointment with her after Carter busted his own lip open during one of his recent fits. He will sometimes throw his entire body down so hard and it seems he does not feel pain in that moment.

 He recently turned 6 years old and due to how delayed he is as well as covid-19, he has remained at Hopebridge full-time this school year. I am hoping next school year we can at least start him part-time in public school and go from there as we want him to have as normal of a life as possible. In the meantime, we count every day that Carter is peaceful as a blessing. The days that have been the toughest have been my cry out to God moments. I have anointed his bedroom with oil, I have laid on his bed and prayed and cried. I hold tight to Psalm 139:14(ESV)- I praise you, for I am fearfully and wonderfully made. And to Jeremiah 29:11(ESV)- For I know the plans I have for you, declares the Lord, plans for welfare and not for evil, to give you a hope and a future. Even though Carter does not always respond to me, I continue to get on his level and pray with him at night and in the morning when he wakes up and over his meals. I sing children's bible songs to him and on occasion he will sing the chorus to Jesus loves me or the B.I.B.L.E on his own. I play worship music at home and in the car. If it is a rough attitude day for him, then I will choose a cd with mellow worship music. He seems to respond the most to my Alan Jackson Precious Memories cd that is filled with the old traditional gospel hymns. Occasionally he will also watch a story from the bible on the bible for kids' app that is on my phone or bible song videos on YouTube. I have hope that he is learning about Jesus's love for him through these resources.

Ephesians 5:19(ESV)- Addressing one another in psalms and hymns and spiritual songs, singing and making melody to the Lord with your heart.

Identifying

 One of the bible studies I participated in was the Armor of God study and that study really helped me to be more aware of the enemy's attacks and the things he used to attack with. I know the wicked one uses our son's tantrum behaviors to target us. He also at times will try and use social media on me. Certain rough days with Carter I will see all the happy (or what appears to be happy) families posing so nicely on their media pages and I have to sometimes fight myself to not feel like, "oh it must be nice." I simply close my social media to avoid those negative feelings. The one time we tried a professional photography studio for family pictures, Carter tried to run and wanted no part of it. It was not a very fun experience. I sometimes feel like we are missing out as we are limited on the public things we can go and do as a family. So yes, at times I've been guilty of feeling negative. But I know if I stay in that negative funk it can turn toxic and God commands me to be thankful.

1 Thessalonians 5:16-18(ESV)- Rejoice always, pray without ceasing, give thanks in ALL circumstances; for this is the will of God in Christ Jesus for you. So, I simply shake off those negative feelings and if possible, remove myself from whatever may be tempting that negative emotion, and ask God's forgiveness. I've even felt blah at times seeing "higher functioning" children with autism that are in school, can communicate, and are progressing nicely. I want so badly for Carter to become higher functioning. He has so much knowledge trapped inside of him just waiting to come out. I know that if we don't give up, he will eventually get there.

Galatians 6:9(NLT)- So let's not get tired of doing what is good. At just the right time we will reap a harvest of blessing if we don't give up.

The enemy may use autism against us, but God causes everything to work for good. (Romans 8:28).

Quarantine and the Emotional Battle

October 26, 2020, I get a phone call from Hopebridge and find out Carter will be required to quarantine for 2 weeks after some therapists from his room have come back positive for COVID-19. Thankfully, they have been wearing a mask at all times as Carter does not wear one. I've tried a couple times to hold a mask up to him, but he quickly slaps it away. I am not surprised because he also will not wear a hat or headphones. I believe it causes something with his sensory sensitivity and I can't force him. Our first week of quarantine was an absolute challenge. Every day from that Tuesday-Friday he had horrible fits, some lasting 2+ hours. Nothing I do seems to correct the behaviors so at one point I simply put in my earbuds and stayed in my bedroom until he calmed down. Other times I sat at the dining room table and cried and pleaded with God to make him stop. I even anointed his forehead one of the mornings when he woke up angry before getting out of bed. I definitely was desperate for some relief from this. Saturday came and Chris was home from work, and it was Halloween. Carter seemed to be in a pretty good mood finally after several bad ones. The weather warmed up and the sun was shining. We were able to spend a decent amount of time playing in the backyard on the sensory type swing we had gotten him the weekend before. We watched Halloween themed children's cartoons which he seemed to enjoy. I dressed him up in his Mario pajama 1-piece costume (the only kind of costume I can get him to wear due to sensory issues) and he checked himself out in the bathroom mirror and laughed with joy. We went to dad for "trick or treat" and he decided to dig his little hands in and grab every single piece of candy which brought us a much-needed laugh. The little moments that make us smile and laugh we hold onto and cherish.

We are currently halfway through our 2nd week of quarantine and so far, the behaviors this week are still happening. One day I tried to get Carter to paint a canvas for an activity to entertain him. Apparently, I chose the wrong color of paint and that set him off, needless to say, he didn't paint that morning and went back to watching his cartoons. Sometimes you have to just pick and choose your battles in order to keep the peace. This second week the weather outside has been really nice and has warmed up, so we were able to get out and go for some walks for a change of scenery. Week 1 I was at my wits end and at times just ready to give up. Week 2 I feel like my mind and emotional state has changed to a more positive and instead of dreading being stuck at home with Carter, I am simply trying to enjoy the time God has allowed for us to have a break from the busyness of life to spend quality time together. I have monitored both Carter as well as my own temperatures each day and we have remained in good health with no symptoms of any sickness. I feel pretty positive that we will remain symptom free and will continue our

normal routines on Monday. I can keep that
promise because I know that the Lord is with us.
Isaiah 41:10(ESV)- Fear not, for I am with you;
be not dismayed, for I am your God; I will
strengthen you, I will help you, I will uphold
you with my righteous right hand.

 I believe that the struggles we have faced and
the struggles going on currently will be used to
help others who God places on our path in the
future. 2 Corinthians 1:3-4(ESV)- Blessed be
the God and Father of our Lord Jesus Christ, the
father of mercies and God of all comfort, who
comforts us in all our affliction, so that we may
be able to comfort those who are in any
affliction, with the comfort with which we
ourselves are comforted by God.

 Until then, we wait patiently and go on the path
in which God leads us and put our hope and
trust in him for his plan is perfect.

Conclusion

 I decided to share my story to bring awareness to others about the difficulty's children with autism and their families face as well as give hope to others starting a journey with autism. I receive my strength through being in a relationship with Christ, spending time in prayer, reading scripture, and singing and listening to worship music. Despite the struggles (John 16:33), at the end of the day, I have peace. If you don't have a relationship with Jesus Christ, simply ask him to come into your heart and your life can be forever changed.
God Bless,

Melissa